HASTEN
THE
KINGDOM

Praying the
O Antiphons of Advent

Mary Winifred, C.A.

A Liturgical Press Book

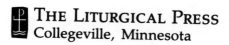

THE LITURGICAL PRESS
Collegeville, Minnesota

Cover design by David Manahan, O.S.B.

Illustrations by Placid Stuckenschneider, O.S.B.

All of the music for the O Antiphons, other than the antiphon on page 46, is from the *Antiphonale Monasticum,* 1934, and has been adapted to English texts by Bartholomew L. Sayles, O.S.B.

1	2	3	4	5	6	7	8

ISBN 0-8146-2363-8

for Edward Nason West

ACKNOWLEDGEMENTS

My thanks to the Community of the Holy Spirit, especially to Sr. Elise, Sr. Emmanuel, Sr. Faith Margaret, and Sr. Catherine Grace for their help and insight; as well as to Madeleine L'Engle.

I am also grateful to Diogenes, Jane, and Timothy Allen; Gurdon and Martha Brewster; Thomas Coffey; Cynthia Frazier; Dolly Frisch; William Loring; Ann Tillman; and Patricia Wallace who helped me by listening, reading, questioning, and offering general encouragement.

CONTENTS

PREFACE

In *Hasten the Kingdom* Sister Mary Winifred has given us a beautiful way to recover the meaning of Advent, a season of awe and hope which has nearly been lost in the hustle and bustle of crowded shops, office parties, and the terrible anxiety that comes from not knowing just what it is for which we are waiting.

Through this book she has offered us a way of attending to the ancient and beautiful O Antiphons through moments of prayer, silence, meditation. What a blessing! What a relief during days in which we ostensibly should be quiet, but are far more often full of noise and exhaustion.

We are not waiting for the birth of Jesus in Bethlehem, for that extraordinary event, which broke ordinary time into fragments, has already happened. The Word, which joyfully shouted all the galaxies into being, left All Power and came silently into the womb of a young girl; there it waited to be born as all of us are born, waited to come into human time, and did so all for love of us mortal creatures. God, within Mary; God, within us. This is an action so wild and wonderful that it strikes terror into many hearts, a terror so great that we try to assuage it either with sentimentality over a tiny baby, or with noise, lest the silence become too much to bear.

But this birth is not what we are waiting for. We remember it in order to understand that that for which we are truly waiting is the second coming, the redemption of all things—we tiny creatures on this little planet, the planet itself, the solar system, our galaxy, the universe.

Traditionally during Advent we are to ponder the four last things: death, judgment, hell, and heaven. It is a formidable prospect. *Hasten the Kingdom* will help us move through the last days of the Church's year with joy and hope. Sister Mary Winifred offers the wisdom of traditional prayers and readings along with her own serene meditations and poems. This little book is full of great insights. If we rest each evening with the O Antiphons as Sister Mary Winifred has presented them, Advent will be for us once again a time of God's great love and hope.

—*Madeleine L'Engle*

Hasten, O Father, the coming of your kingdom; and grant that we, your servants, who now live by faith, may with joy behold your Son at his coming in glorious majesty; even Jesus Christ, our only Mediator and Advocate. Amen.[1]

The Book of Common Prayer

INTRODUCTION

Advent. A time of waiting and watching and preparation. A time, if we are not careful, of rampant materialism and tension that looks forward only to a too-secularized and too-commercialized Christmas holiday. On the other hand, Advent can be a time like no other—a time in which we pause and ask Christ into our hearts, invite God into our world.

But who is this God who comes to us and enters into our life? How do we invite God into our lives? How do we know Christ Jesus? One way to discover Christ and to pray for God's coming is to use the ancient prayers of the early church together with a present-day understanding of what Christ's coming will mean for us.

The well-known carol, "O come, O come, Emmanuel," provides just such a passageway linking the old and the new:

O come, O come, Emmanuel,
And ransom captive Israel,
That mourns in lonely exile here
Until the Son of God appear.
Rejoice! Rejoice! Emmanuel
Shall come to thee, O Israel!

O come, thou Wisdom from on high.
Who ord'rest all things mightily;
To us the path of knowledge show,
And teach us in her ways to go.
Rejoice! Rejoice! Emmanuel
Shall come to thee, O Israel!

O come, O come, thou Lord of might,
Who to thy tribes on Sinai's height
In ancient times didst give the law,
In cloud, and majesty, and awe.
Rejoice! Rejoice! Emmanuel
Shall come to thee, O Israel!

O come, thou Rod of Jesse's stem,
From every foe deliver them
That trust thy mighty power to save,
And give them vict'ry o'er the grave.
Rejoice! Rejoice! Emmanuel
Shall come to thee, O Israel!

O come, thou Key of David, come,
And open wide our heav'nly home;
Make safe the way that leads on high,
And close the path to misery.
Rejoice! Rejoice! Emmanuel
Shall come to thee, O Israel!

O come, thou Day-spring from on high
And cheer us by thy drawing nigh;
Disperse the gloomy clouds of night
And death's dark shadow put to flight.
Rejoice! Rejoice! Emmanuel
Shall come to thee, O Israel!

O come, Desire of nations, bind
In one the hearts of all mankind;
Bid thou our sad divisions cease,
And be thyself our King of Peace.
Rejoice! Rejoice! Emmanuel
Shall come to thee, O Israel![1]

The carol's familiar names for Christ are based on the Advent
Antiphons—the "Great O's"—which date back possibly to the sixth
century. These antiphons—short devotional texts chanted before
and after a psalm or canticle—were sung before and after the
Magnificat, the Song of Mary, at Vespers from December 16

through December 23. Each of the antiphons greets the Messiah and ends with a petition of hope.

Later, another O Antiphon was included, O Virgo virginum— O Virgin of Virgins—sung on December 23rd. With this addition, the antiphons were begun on December 16th.

The simple refrain of the carol, "Rejoice! Rejoice! Emmanuel shall come to thee, O Israel!" sets the tone for this Advent time of waiting and expectation.

Just as "O come, O come, Emmanuel" retains a significant place in our Advent worship, the Great O Antiphons are still sung each December in monasteries and convents. The wording of the antiphons may have been updated and redirected to fit more modern music and language, but the essence of the prayers is the same.

We ask God to come as Wisdom to make us prudent, as Adonai, the Lord, to save and redeem us, as the Root of Jesse to deliver us into love, as the Key of David to bring freedom, as Day-spring to shed light and life, as the King of nations to give peace, and as Emmanuel to offer hope and bring salvation. The final antiphon, addressed to Mary on the Vigil of Christmas, is an acknowledgement on our part that at last the mystery of the Incarnation will always be just that—a mystery.

The following meditations are based on the Great O Antiphons, together with their scriptural texts. At the close of each day's text there is a prayer or restructuring of the antiphon in poetic free form. The worship format is designed to be used by individuals or small groups, in the evening or at another convenient time. Participants are encouraged to take part as fully as possible by sharing responsibilities for readings and contributing their own reflections.

O WIS - DOM, * you came forth from the mouth of the Most High and reach from one end of the earth to the oth-er, might-i-ly and sweet-ly or-der-ing all things. O come and teach us the way of pru - dence.

4

DECEMBER 16

OPENING PRAYER

O gracious light,
pure brightness of the everliving Father in heaven
O Jesus Christ, holy and blessed!
Now as we come to the setting of the sun,
and our eyes behold the vesper light,
we sing your praises O God: Father, Son, and Holy Spirit.
You are worthy at all times to be praised by happy voices,
O Son of God, O Giver of life,
and to be glorified through all the worlds.

READINGS

For the Lord gives wisdom;
    from his mouth come
        knowledge and
        understanding;
Then you will understand
    righteousness and justice
    and equity, every good path.

Proverbs 2:6, 9-11

Because the spirit of the Lord
 has filled the world,
and that which holds all things
 together knows what is said.

Wisdom 1:7

"O God of my ancestors and
 Lord of my mercy,
who have made all things by your word. . . .
With you is wisdom, she who
 knows your works
and was present when you made
 the world;
she understands what is pleasing
 in your sight
and what is right according to
 your commandments.
Send her forth from the holy
 heavens,
and from the throne of your
 glory send her,
that she may labor at my side,
and that I may learn what is
 pleasing to you.
For she knows and understands
 all things,
and she will guide me wisely in
 my actions
and guard me with her glory.

Wisdom 9:1, 9-11

THE SONG OF MARY

Antiphon: O Wisdom, you came forth from the mouth of the Most High and reach from one end of the earth to the other, mightily and sweetly ordering all things. O come and teach us the way of prudence.

My soul proclaims the greatness of the Lord,
 my spirit rejoices in God my Savior;

for he has looked with favor on his lowly servant.
From this day all generations will call me blessed:
   the Almighty has done great things for me,
   and holy is his Name.
He has mercy on those who fear him
   in every generation.
He has shown the strength of his arm,
   he has scattered the proud in their conceit.
He has cast down the mighty from their thrones,
   and has lifted up the lowly.
He has filled the hungry with good things,
   and the rich he has sent away empty.
He has come to the help of his servant Israel,
   for he has remembered his promise of mercy,
The promise he made to our fathers,
   to Abraham and his children for ever.
Glory to the Father, and to the Son, and to the Holy Spirit:
   as it was in the beginning, is now, and will be for ever. Amen.

Antiphon: O Wisdom, you came forth from the mouth of the Most
High and reach from one end of the earth to the other, mightily
and sweetly ordering all things. O come and teach us the way of
prudence.

THE LORD'S PRAYER

Our Father in heaven,
   hallowed be your Name,
   your kingdom come,
   your will be done,
   on earth as in heaven.
Give us today our daily bread.
Forgive us our sins
   as we forgive those who sin against us.
Save us from the time of trial
   and deliver us from evil.
For the kingdom, the power, and the glory are yours,
   now and for ever. Amen.

MEDITATION

In his book, *The Far-Spent Night,* Edward West pointed out that the first thing needed in preparing to meet the Lord is prudence or "good sense." "It is good sense," he said, "which makes the disobedient listen to the wisdom of the just. It is good sense which makes [us] cope with the whole of life as a unit. It is good sense applied to every area of living which is the outward and visible sign of an inner integrity. In short, it means to have understanding, but it is an understanding of wisdom."[1]

In the context of the Old Testament, wisdom is always a gift from God, rather than some skill or knowledge that we can gain for ourselves. In the context of the New Testament, wisdom is a person. Wisdom is *who* Christ is and *what* Christ does. Wisdom is often thought of as feminine—as the Greek "Sophia"—through which we access a deeper knowledge and understanding of God, not only as creator, but also as nurturer and sustainer. Attributing more feminine characteristics to God, far from diminishing our view, enhances and enlivens our personal relationship with God, and assists in deepening our spirituality. A new light is shed on the action of the gospels in our lives and in our relationships. And there is an eternal quality about wisdom in that it was presented to us at the beginning of time, reaching through the present and into the future.

It is when wisdom truly comes to us that we will have the prudence—the good sense—to listen and to follow where Christ leads. In asking Christ to come as Wisdom, we are praying for a unity in our life that will draw us into purpose and vision, and away from fragmentation and unproductivity. The Wisdom that is Christ may well lead us in the ways of the just: into compassion, concern, peace, justice, and love.

O Wisdom,
>   gift on the breath of creation,
>   measurer of the earth and seas,
>   singer of paths for stars and planets in the heavens,
>   holder of all things together
>   since before time and forever.

My sister, my friend,
as the Spirit of the Lord fills the whole world,
and as you know every word that is said,
come as mentor and guide:
  so I'll delight in knowledge,
claim intuition and understanding for my own,
discern, learn
  what his advent holds for me.
O Wisdom, my sister,
  let us lean close, laugh and weep together,
  be one with each other as we shout our whispered
    greeting
to the Lord of life.

CLOSING PRAYER

O Lord, mercifully receive the prayers of your people who call upon you, and grant that they may know and understand what things they ought to do, and also that they may have the grace and power to faithfully accomplish them; through Jesus Christ our Lord, who lives and reigns with you and the Holy Spirit, one God, now and for ever. Amen.[2]

O   A - DO - NAI * and Lead - er of the

house of Is - ra - el,   you ap - peared to Mo - ses in the fire

of the burn - ing bush   and gave him the

law   on Si - nai.   O   come and re -   deem

rit.

us with   an   out - stretched arm.

O ADONAI

DECEMBER 17

OPENING PRAYER

O gracious Light,
pure brightness of the everliving Father in heaven,
O Jesus Christ, holy and blessed!
Now as we come to the setting of the sun,
and our eyes behold the vesper light,
we sing your praises, O God: Father, Son, and Holy Spirit.
You are worthy at all times to be praised by happy voices,
O Son of God, O Giver of life,
and to be glorified through all the worlds.

READINGS

There the angel of the Lord appeared to him in a flame of fire
out of a bush; he looked, and the bush was blazing, yet it was
not consumed. . . . When the Lord saw that he had turned
aside to see, God called to him out of the bush, "Moses, Moses!"
And he said, "Here I am. . . ." He said further, "I am the
God of your father, the God of Abraham, the God of Isaac, and
the God of Jacob." And Moses hid his face, for he was afraid
to look at God.

Exodus 3:2, 4, 6

11

Then God spoke all these words:

I am the Lord Your God, who brought you out of the land of Egypt, out of the house of slavery; you shall have no other gods before me.

Exodus 20:1-2

The Lord has bared his holy arm
before the eyes of all the nations;
and all the ends of the earth shall see
the salvation of our God.

Isaiah 52:10

THE SONG OF MARY

Antiphon: O Adonai and Leader of the house of Israel, you appeared to Moses in the fire of the burning bush and gave him the law on Sinai. O come and redeem us with an outstretched arm.

My soul glorifies the Lord,
and my spirit rejoices in God my Savior,
  for he has been mindful of the humble state of his servant.
From now on generations will call me blessed,
  for the Mighty One has done great things for me—
  holy is his name.
His mercy extends to those who fear him,
  from generation to generation.
He has performed mighty deeds with his arm;
  he has scattered those who are proud in their inmost thoughts.
He has brought down the rulers from their thrones,
  but has lifted up the humble.
He has filled the hungry with good things
  and sent the rich away empty.
He has helped his servant Israel,
  remembering to be merciful
to Abraham and to his descendants forever,
  even as he has said to our fathers.
Glory to the Father, and to the son, and to the Holy Spirit:
  as it was in the beginning, is now, and will be forever. Amen.

Antiphon: O Adonai and Leader of the house of Israel, you appeared to Moses in the fire of the burning bush and gave him the law on Sinai. O come and redeem us with an outstretched arm.

THE LORD'S PRAYER

Our Father in heaven,
　hallowed be your Name,
　your kingdom come,
　your will be done,
　on earth as in heaven.
Give us today our daily bread.
Forgive us our sins
　as we forgive those who sin against us.
Save us from the time of trial
　and deliver us from evil.
For the kingdom, the power, and the glory are yours,
　now and for ever. Amen.

MEDITATION

In ancient Israel the title "Adonai" was used in place of the name of God, "I am who I am"—I was and I will be. Adonai is the lord and leader—the one who would redeem or buy back Israel's freedom from slavery.

When God called from the burning bush to Moses, it was with a message of God's self-revelation, of strength, and of freedom. Moses was to lead the Israelites from Egypt into a new land, but God would go before them as protection and a shield. It would be by God's might and power that Israel would be saved, not by Moses' strength or cleverness. God's identity and character would be made known in the events of the exodus from Egypt.

As it was necessary to understand the meaning of "prudence" in order to welcome Wisdom, so we must delve into the deeper meaning of "freedom" if we are to greet Christ as Adonai. In his book, *Three Outsiders*, Diogenes Allen wrote of the relationship of Christianity and human freedom: "Christianity will inevitably appear to be hostile to human freedom. For even though it promises human fulfillment and eternal joy, it claims that to enter the kingdom of God requires an act of renunciation. . . . [But it is

13

a] superficial optimism which claims that with more possessions, better education, better health, a longer life, and more personal liberty, human beings can be made happy. It is true that deprivation makes us miserable, but . . . to have these things is not sufficient to make us happy. Only God can give us fullness because only he has an inexhaustible fullness. By yielding to him we can become free of our bondage to boredom, anxiety, and overdependence on things which cannot give us happiness."[1]

Just as certainly as God spoke to Moses in the burning bush, God also speaks as leader to us today. As Israel's freedom from slavery in Egypt was dependent on following God, so our true "freedom" is available only if we belong to God. Moses and ancient Israel understood God's redemption as release from captivity in Egypt, freedom from slavery, acquired at the outstretched arm of a warrior. Ironically, that freedom is only a shadow of the true freedom of belonging to God. We do not escape from captivity because of our strength and cleverness; Christ the redeemer, our Adonai, buys us back from captivity because of his sanctifying love. It is only by Christ's arm outstretched on a cross that we gain our freedom. God's identity and character are made known to us in the events of the incarnation.

The challenges of this Advent season may lie not only in naming the forces of our slavery and captivity, but also in discovering our own "burning bush" images, in hearing the voice of God—Adonai—leading us to freedom.

> O Lord and leader,
>   I'd see and understand you in an unburned bush,
>   . . . if I were Moses.
>   You, a fiery warrior,
>   bringer of law and order;
>   deliverer, designer,
>   strong and powerful.
>   Leader of the led and lord of all.
> The God of Abraham,
>   the God of Isaac,
>   and the God of Jacob.
>   . . . if I were Moses.

As it is,
>You are more obvious to me
>>in the laughing eyes of children,
>>in the sick, the homeless, street people,
>>the prisoners:
>>>guilty and not guilty.
>>Unexpected, almost uninvited,
>>bringer of joy and tears,
>>questions and courage and comfort.

The God of Miriam,
>the God of Sarah,
>the God of Rebecca,
>even the God of Leah and Rachel,
>the God of Naomi,
>and most definitely the God of Ruth.
>. . . like Moses, yes.
You are my God,
>But, my God, for me
>>your redeeming arm is outstretched on a cross.

CLOSING PRAYER

Almighty and everlasting God, whose will it is to restore all things in your well-beloved Son, the King of kings and Lord of lords: Mercifully grant that the peoples of the earth, divided and enslaved by sin, may be freed and brought together under his most gracious rule; who lives and reigns with you and the Holy Spirit, one God, now and for ever. Amen.[2]

O   ROOT OF JES – SE, * you stand
as an en-sign to the peo – ples; be-fore you
kings will shut their mouths   and na-tions
will bow   in   wor-ship.   O   come and de –
liv – er   us   and do   not   tar – ry.

O STOCK OF JESSE

DECEMBER 18

OPENING PRAYER

O gracious Light,
pure brightness of the everliving Father in heaven,
O Jesus Christ, holy and blessed!
Now as we come to the setting of the sun,
and our eyes behold the vesper light,
we sing your praises, O God: Father, Son, and Holy Spirit.
You are worthy at all times to be praised by happy voices,
O Son of God, O Giver of life,
and to be glorified through all the worlds.

READINGS

A shoot shall come out from the stump of Jesse,
and a branch shall grow out of his roots.
The spirit of the Lord shall rest on him,
the spirit of wisdom and understanding,
the spirit of counsel and might,
the spirit of knowledge and the fear of the Lord.
His delight shall be in the fear of the Lord.
He shall not judge by what his eyes see,
or decide by what his ears hear;
but with righteousness he shall judge the poor,

and decide with equity for the meek of the earth.
On that day the root of Jesse
shall stand as a signal to the peoples;
the nations shall inquire of him,
and his dwelling shall be glorious.
On that day the Lord will extend his hand yet a second time
to recover the remnant that is left of his people.

Isaiah 11:1-4a, 10-11a

See, my servant shall prosper;
he shall be exalted and lifted up, and shall be very high.
So he shall startle many nations;
kings shall shut their mouths because of him;
for that which had not been told them they shall see,
and that which they had not heard they shall contemplate.

Isaiah 52:13, 15

THE SONG OF MARY

Antiphon: O Root of Jesse, you stand as an ensign to the peoples;
before you kings will shut their mouths and nations will bow in
worship. O come and deliver us and do not tarry.

My soul magnifies the Lord,
    and my spirit rejoices in God my Savior,
for he has looked with favor on the lowliness of his servant.
    Surely, from now on all generations will call me blessed;
for the Mighty One has done great things for me,
    and holy is his name.
His mercy is for those who fear him
    from generation to generation.
He has shown strength with his arm;
    he has scattered the proud in the thoughts of their hearts.
He has brought down the powerful from their thrones,
    and lifted up the lowly;
he has filled the hungry with good things,
    and sent the rich away empty.
He has helped his servant Israel,
    in remembrance of his mercy,

18

according to the promise he made to our ancestors,
to Abraham and to his descendants forever.

Antiphon: O Root of Jesse, you stand as an ensign to the peoples;
before you kings will shut their mouths and nations will bow in
worship. O come and deliver us and do not tarry.

THE LORD'S PRAYER

Our Father in heaven,
hallowed be your Name,
your kingdom come,
your will be done,
on earth as in heaven.
Give us today our daily bread.
Forgive us our sins
as we forgive those who sin against us.
Save us from the time of trial
and deliver us from evil.
For the kingdom, the power, and the glory are yours,
now and for ever. Amen.

MEDITATION

As Adonai is our lord and leader, it is the Root of Jesse that
delivers us into love for each other—not a love that molds another
into our own image, but a love that sees each one through the
eyes of God. It is because Christ comes as a sign for all creation
that king and servant are equal, Jew and gentile are alike in their
search; everyone is holy.

Actually we all are equal in the sight of God. Too often we see
the "accidents" of life—one's appearance, talents, mannerisms—
as if they were the measure of the person, when, in reality,
stripped of all these accidental characteristics, we are, each of
us, the same.

Many years ago, this light-hearted story was reported in a local
newspaper: Queen Elizabeth II was attending a horse show when
an over-zealous police officer cautioned a young boy nearby,

"You're standing too close to the Queen." The unrecognized prince responded innocently, "But she's my mother!"

At the other end of the socio-economic spectrum is a more sobering story of equality told by Howard Stowe, the former rector of St. Ignatius' Episcopal Church in New York City. After almost an hour of driving around in snow and heavy, late-afternoon traffic looking for a parking place on Manhattan's crowded upper West Side, he had at last discovered a just-large-enough space about two blocks from the church's front door. Dirty snow and slush were piled from the curb onto the day's uncollected garbage bags and trash cans. He had somehow eased his car into the parking space, but had to push the car door heavily against the trash and ice slush in order to get out of the car. Suddenly from one of the black plastic bags came a voice, "Hey, Mister, be careful. I'm a man; I'm not garbage!"

Queen, prince, street person, priest—everyone is holy. And it is Christ himself who not only leads us into mutual concern and compassion, but also reminds us just how holy each one is. Charles deFoucauld summarized this truth, "I do not think there is a gospel phrase which has made a deeper impression on me and transformed my life more than this one: 'Insofar as you did this to one of the least of these . . . you did it to me.' One has only to think that these words were spoken by the uncreated Truth, who also said, 'This is my body . . . This is my blood.' "[1]

It is with the coming of Christ that the groundwork for our union with God is begun, but we will only be able to grow in this union when we are in communion and in community with others. Christ comes as the sign that all are welcome.

O Root of Jesse
   The nations—all the nations—seek you.
   And kings—even kings and rulers, prophets and seers—
      even kings and queens,
     who usually understand and make pronouncements—
  even kings stand speechless,
    dumbfounded,
      witness to something
        they cannot begin to imagine: God!

God, himself, a sign of the people—
  the average, ordinary, everyday, all people.
God himself a sign
  that the people are holy . . .
    wholly wrapped in the Spirit
      of wisdom and insight,
      of counsel and power,
      of knowledge and awe,
      of godliness, itself—
    all the people are holy.
O Root of Jesse
  stand as a signal,
    as a sign to the people
  of the holiness of God,
  of the holiness of us all.

CLOSING PRAYER

O God, you have taught us to keep all your commandments by loving you and our neighbor: Grant us the grace of your Holy Spirit, that we may be devoted to you with our whole heart and united to one another with pure affection; through Jesus Christ our Lord, who lives and reigns with you and the Holy Spirit, one God, for ever and ever. Amen.[2]

O KEY OF DA - VID * and Scep-
ter of the house of Is-ra-el, you o - pen and no one
can close; you close and no one can
o - pen. O come and bring cap-tives out
of the pris-on house, those who sit in
dark ness and the shad - ow of death.

O KEY OF DAVID

DECEMBER 19

OPENING PRAYER

O gracious Light,
pure brightness of the everliving Father in heaven,
O Jesus Christ, holy and blessed!
Now as we come to the setting of the sun,
and our eyes behold the vesper light,
we sing your praises, O God: Father, Son, and Holy Spirit.
You are worthy at all times to be praised by happy voices,
O Son of God, O Giver of life,
and to be glorified through all the worlds.

READINGS

I am the Lord, I have called you in righteousness,
  I have taken you by the hand and kept you;
I have given you as a covenant to the people,
  a light to the nations,
  to open the eyes that are blind,
to bring out the prisoners from the dungeon,
  from the prison those who sit in darkness.

Isaiah 42:6-7

Then they cried to the Lord in their trouble,
and he saved them from their distress;
he brought them out of darkness and gloom,
and broke their bonds asunder.

Psalm 107:13-14

I see him, but not now;
I behold him, but not near—
a star shall come out of Jacob,
and a scepter shall rise out of Israel.

Numbers 24:17a

I will place on his shoulder the key of the house of David;
he shall open, and no one shall shut; he shall shut, and no one
shall open.

Isaiah 22:22

THE SONG OF MARY

Antiphon: O Key of David and Scepter of the house of Israel, you
open and no one can close; you close and no one can open. O come
and bring captives out of the prison house, those who sit in darkness and the shadow of death.

How I rejoice in God my Savior!
For he took notice of his lowly servant girl,
and now generation after generation forever shall call me
blest of God.
For he, the mighty Holy One, has done great things to me.
His mercy goes on from generation to generation, to all
who reverence him.
How powerful is his mighty arm!
How he scatters the proud and haughty ones!
He has torn princes from their thrones and exalted the lowly.
He has satisfied the hungry hearts and sent the rich away
with empty hands.
And how he has helped his servant Israel!
He has not forgotten his promise to be merciful.
For he promised our fathers—Abraham and his children—
to be merciful to them forever.

Glory to the Father, and the Son, and to the Holy Spirit:
as it was in the beginning, is now, and will be forever.
Amen.

Antiphon: O Key of David and Scepter of the house of Israel, you open and no one can close; you close and no one can open. O come and bring captives out of the prison house, those who sit in darkness and the shadow of death.

THE LORD'S PRAYER

Our Father in heaven,
hallowed be your Name,
your kingdom come,
your will be done,
on earth as in heaven.
Give us today our daily bread.
Forgive us our sins
as we forgive those who sin against us.
Save us from the time of trial
and deliver us from evil.
For the kingdom, the power, and the glory are yours,
now and for ever. Amen.

MEDITATION

Only those who have been incarcerated can know fully the isolation and dehumanization of being physically locked in prison—the humiliation of strip searches, the desolation of loneliness, the fear of physical and sexual abuse from officers and other inmates, the terror of nightmares, the often unabated guilt and anger over past mistakes. It is no wonder that the scriptural texts for today's antiphon refer to prisons as an analogy for darkness and captivity, and then also echo a hope of future release and freedom.

It is only because Christ comes as the Key of David that prison can be also a place of transformation. In his book, *Summons To Serve,* Richard Atherton shared his vision of one redeeming influence of prison life. Atherton, for many years a prison chaplain in England, knew first hand of the harshness of prison life, and his observations are demanding, but utterly trustworthy as well. "Using the imagery of Scripture, I like to think of prison as a desert; a place where the human spirit may be purified and ennobled but, alas, more easily twisted and damaged; a place that is often threatening and almost always unpredictable; a place where faith is put to the test—the faith of the inmates, but that of their pastor too; a place of loneliness and powerlessness and frustration, where [one] begins to feel . . . the truth of our Lord's words: 'Without me you can do nothing' (John 15:5); and so ultimately a place of encounter with God."[1]

For those who have not experienced life in an actual prison, there are, nevertheless, other "prison" experiences—prisons that can be rigorously isolating and dehumanizing in their own way. There is a prison of fear and hate, a prison of anger, and a prison of resistance to openness and change; there is a prison of physical limitation and disability, of painful relationships, of difficult employment, and of unemployment. Most often we lock ourselves into these prisons; with Christ, however, even here we can encounter God. And it is this encounter that will begin the unlocking, opening process to freedom.

The freedom that Christ—the Key of David—brings is an openness to new ideas and concepts, and a welcoming invitation to change, grow, and develop. It offers a path away from death, toward life. In a translation of 18th century words, T. A. Lacey wrote,

> O come, thou Lord of David's Key!
> The royal door fling wide and free;
> Safeguard for us the heaven-ward road,
> And bar the way to death's abode.[2]

It is in Christ's advent that the way to heaven is forevermore unlocked for us.

But there is a second phrase in this antiphon as well: "you shut and no one can open." This statement may be understood as God's closing of one path in our lives in order to lead or encourage us in another direction; or it may be understood as Christ's forever closing off to us the way to eternal darkness and death. But I prefer to believe that this phrase holds yet another secret of the spiritual life. It is when Christ comes that the justification for mere self-centeredness and self-serving is forever closed. In becoming human, God not only opens the way of freedom, but also shuts the door for individual isolation. At a basic level we too now may, in fact even *must*, identify with others beyond ourselves. We will be held accountable for our relationships with others. To paraphrase a statement by Abraham Heschel, we now encounter God and humanity in one thought, suffering in ourselves the harms and injuries done to others. Through this practice, compassion becomes our greatest passion, love and defiance of despair our greatest strengths. If we are truly living a Christian life, avoidance and neglect become options unavailable to us.

O Key of David,
    come,
    unlock my prison of self-distrust and fear,
        of secrecy and doubt,
        of injustice and unkindness.
Unlock my blindness
    to the splendor and glory of your light.
Unlock my deafness
    to the melody of the world
        and the harmony of the universe.
Unlock my stumbling lameness
    to the dance of your life.
Unlock my depression and gloom
    to the majesty and gentleness of your love.

CLOSING PRAYER

Set us free, O God, from the bondage of our sins, and give us the liberty of that abundant life which you have made known to us in your Son our Savior Jesus Christ, who lives and reigns with you, in the unity of the Holy Spirit, one God, now and for ever. Amen.[3]

O RIS - ING DAWN, * bright - ness

of the Light E - ter - nal and Sun of Right -

eous - ness, O come and en -

light - en those who sit in dark -

rit.

ness and the shad - ow of death.

O DAWN

DECEMBER 20

OPENING PRAYER

O gracious Light,
pure brightness of the everliving Father in heaven,
O Jesus Christ, holy and blessed!
Now as we come to the setting of the sun,
and our eyes behold the vesper light,
we sing your praises, O God: Father, Son, and Holy Spirit.
You are worthy at all times to be praised by happy voices,
O Son of God, O Giver of life,
and to be glorified through all the worlds.

READINGS

The people who walked in darkness
  have seen a great light;
those who lived in a land of deep darkness—
  on them a light has shined.

Isaiah 9:2

The sun shall no longer be your light by day,
nor for brightness shall the moon
  give light to you by night;

29

but the Lord will be your everlasting light,
   and your God will be your glory.
Your sun shall no more go down,
   or your moon withdraw itself;
for the Lord will be your everlasting light,
and your days of mourning shall be ended.

Isaiah 60:19-20

For she is a reflection of eternal light,
a spotless mirror of the working of God,
and an image of his goodness.

Wisdom 7:26

But for you who revere my name the sun of righteousness
shall rise, with healing in its wings.

Malachi 4:2

And you, child, will be called the prophet of the Most High;
   for you will go before the Lord to prepare his ways,
to give knowledge of salvation to his people
   by the forgiveness of their sins.
By the tender mercy of our God,
   the dawn from on high will break upon us,
to give light to those who sit in darkness and in the shadow
      of death,
   to guide our feet into the way of peace.

Luke 1:76-79

THE SONG OF MARY

Antiphon: O Rising Dawn, brightness of the Light Eternal and
Sun of Righteousness, O come and enlighten those who sit in
darkness and the shadow of death.

My soul proclaims the greatness of the Lord
and my spirit exults in God my Savior;
because he has looked upon his lowly handmaid.
Yes, from this day forward all generations will call me blessed,
for the Almighty has done great things for me.
Holy is his name,
and his mercy reaches from age to age for those who fear him.

He has shown the power of his arm,
he has routed the proud of heart.
He has pulled down princes from their thrones and exalted
the lowly.
The hungry he has filled with good things, the rich sent
empty away.
He has come to the help of Israel his servant, mindful of his
mercy—according to the promise he made to our ancestors—
of his mercy to Abraham and to his descendants for ever.
Glory to the Father, and to the Son, and to the Holy Spirit:
as it was in the beginning, is now, and will be forever. Amen.

Antiphon: O Rising Dawn, brightness of the Light Eternal and
Sun of Righteousness, O come and enlighten those who sit in
darkness and the shadow of death.

THE LORD'S PRAYER

Our Father in heaven,
hallowed be your Name,
your kingdom come,
your will be done,
on earth as in heaven.
Give us today our daily bread.
Forgive us our sins
as we forgive those who sin against us.
Save us from the time of trial
and deliver us from evil.
For the kingdom, the power, and the glory are yours,
now and for ever. Amen.

MEDITATION

The Day-Spring or Dawn is most surely the bringer of light after
darkness, and is the bringer of life as well as light. Light and life
in this context become the freedom of identity. In *The Far-Spent
Night* Edward West explains, "It means that there is a chance for
each individual human being to be a person instead of a pawn
pushed by events and appetites over destiny's chessboard. Jesus

is in himself the knowledge of this salvation, and the Spirit's task through the Church is to see that all are exposed to it. This is the light which can permeate into the dark recesses of the soul, into the dark places of the mind, and set [us] free. To know God through Christ and in Christ is to be the present possessor of eternal life. As light conquers darkness, so life conquers death. We are already that which we are becoming."[1]

We who live in an era that has almost constant electrical lighting can only vaguely imagine the darkness of nights without artificial light. And yet none of us escapes the "darkness" of confusion, misunderstanding, and fear of the unknown or known. Verses of an ancient hymn, sung in the rays of early morning Epiphany light, hint at the inner darkness that is dispelled by the dawn of Christ's coming:

Remain with us, O Lord of light,
Remove the darkness of the night,
From each one wash away all sin,
Grant blessedness and health within.[2]

Many years ago I encountered the energy and vitality of the dawn, of Christ as Day-Spring. I was tired after working long hours on a project that seemed as though it would never come to fruition. A friend had invited me to spend a few days at her home on the New Jersey shore and, one morning, after much encouragement on her part, we got up early to see the sunrise over the ocean. The morning was dark and the misty breeze that hit our faces was uncomfortably chilly. As we watched in silence, suddenly from the edge of the water's horizon came the huge golden roundness of the sun, lifting my tiredness and depression. And it is in just this, often unexpected, surprising way that Christ the Day-Spring enlightens our souls and spirits.

The light of Christ's coming reveals the life that is already present in each one of us.

O Day-Spring,
    dawn of day,
        bright clearness of the light:
Sometimes, in the very early morning,

I watch for your coming
  to unravel the darkness,
  to unhide the unknown,
  to unmask the shapes and shadows of the night;
And in your sun-brilliant shining
    to discover the secrets of righteousness and justice,
    to discern and learn that where you are,
      there is no shadow,
      no darkness,
      no death.

CLOSING PRAYER

Almighty God, pour upon us the new light of your incarnate Word, that this light, enkindled in our hearts, may shine forth in our lives; through Jesus Christ our Lord, who lives and reigns with you, in the unity of the Holy Spirit, one God, now and forever. Amen.[3]

O   KING OF THE NA   –   TIONS *

and the De - sire of them all, you are   the Cor - ner-

stone   who makes both   one.   O

come and save   the crea - tures   whom you fash - ioned

out of clay.

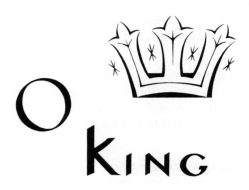

O KING

DECEMBER 21

OPENING PRAYER

O gracious Light,
pure brightness of the everliving Father in heaven,
O Jesus Christ, holy and blessed!
Now as we come to the setting of the sun,
and our eyes behold the vesper light,
we sing your praises, O God: Father, Son, and Holy Spirit.
You are worthy at all times to be praised by happy voices,
O Son of God, O Giver of life,
and to be glorified through all the worlds.

READINGS

. . . therefore thus says the Lord God,
"See, I am laying in Zion a foundation stone,
   a tested stone,
a precious cornerstone, a sure foundation."

Isaiah 28:16

Who would not fear you, O King of nations?
  For that is your due;

among all the wise ones of the nations
and in all their kingdoms
there is no one like you.

Jeremiah 10:7

Come to him, a living stone, though rejected by mortals yet chosen
and precious in God's sight, and like living stones, let yourselves
be built into a spiritual house, to be a holy priesthood, to offer
spiritual sacrifices acceptable to God through Jesus Christ. For
it stands in scripture:

"See, I am laying in Zion a stone,
a cornerstone chosen and precious;
and whoever believes in him will not be put to shame."

1 Peter 2:4-6

Elihu answered . . .:
"But now, hear my speech, O Job,
and listen to all my words.
See, before God I am as you are;
I too was formed from a piece of clay."

Job 33:1, 6

THE SONG OF MARY

Antiphon: O King of the nations and the Desire of them all, you
are the Cornerstone who makes both one. O come and save the
creatures whom you fashioned out of clay.

Tell out, my soul, the greatness of the Lord,
rejoice, rejoice, my spirit, in God my savior;
so tenderly has he looked upon his servant,
humble as she is.
For, from this day forth,
all generations will count me blessed,
so wonderfully has he dealt with me,
the Lord, the Mighty One.
His name is Holy;
his mercy is from generation to generation
toward those who fear him;

the deeds his own right arm have done
   disclose his might:
the arrogant of heart and mind he has put to rout,
he has torn imperial powers from their thrones,
   but the humble has been lifted high.
The hungry he has satisfied with good things,
   the rich sent empty away.
He has ranged himself at the side of Israel his servant;
   firm in his promise to our forefathers,
he has not forgotten to show mercy to Abraham
   and his children's children, for ever.

Antiphon: O King of the nations and the Desire of them all, you are the Cornerstone who makes both one. O come and save the creatures whom you fashioned out of clay.

THE LORD'S PRAYER

Our Father in heaven,
   hallowed be your Name,
   your kingdom come,
   your will be done,
   on earth as in heaven.
Give us today our daily bread.
Forgive us our sins
   as we forgive those who sin against us.
Save us from the time of trial
   and deliver us from evil.
For the kingdom, the power, and the glory are yours,
   now and for ever. Amen.

MEDITATION

The concepts behind "king" and "kingdom" are not easily translatable into our everyday experience, and ideas of royal rights and privileges are uncomfortable for many of us who live in a democracy. Christ as the "King of Nations" only becomes understandable when we realize that his is a kingdom of righteousness and justice, of peace and gentleness. We will recognize the reign of God's kingdom by its righteousness and peace:

When the aged walk with gladness
  In a city bathed in light,
When the races know no sadness
  In the waning of their might,
When the very earth is ringing
  From the temple to the sod,
With the sound of children singing
  Then its peace was born of God.[1]

God's reign is not only the desire of nations, the peace that all nations long for, but also is in itself the foundation and cornerstone of all goodness.

Cornerstones are significant architecturally for they are the connecting joiners of otherwise unstable walls. But they are also important historically, often bearing the date of the building and the architect's name. Stones can also represent social and emotional ties. In one of the buildings at the Community of the Holy Spirit's "Melrose" convent in Brewster, New York, there is a small carved stone from Melrose Abbey in Scotland which serves as a constant reminder of their heritage and theological roots. It is only when Christ comes that the peace and wholeness we long for, and the stability and connectedness needed to attain it, are both actualized.

Derek Kidner, in his commentary on Isaiah, pointed out that the cornerstone is God (Isa 8:14) which is also laid by God—and that it is in Christ that the two metaphors are joined. God is at once salvation itself, and also the means to salvation. Christ, the King of Nations, is salvation itself, while at the same time being the means of salvation.

O King—
  King and Desire of the Nations,
made one by the cornerstone
  of your coming,
  of your being.
    How can it be?
The cornerstone rejected,
  misused as rubble for rocks and stones
  to hurl and smash.

They didn't understand then
   (and often we don't now)
  that cornerstones are
    for fastening onto,
    for building up,
    for foundations and transformation.
Come, O King,
      Desire of the nations,
      Cornerstone.
Save for us, formed of clay,
   the opportunity of being transformed by your peace.

CLOSING PRAYER

Almighty and everlasting God, in Christ you have revealed your
glory among the nations: Preserve the works of your mercy that
we may persevere with steadfast faith in the confession of your
Name; through Jesus Christ our Lord, who lives and reigns with
you and the Holy Spirit, one God, for ever and ever. Amen.[2]

O E - MAN - U - EL, * our King and Law - giv - er, the Ex - pect - ed of the na - tions and the Sav - ior of them all, O come and save us, O Lord our God.

EMMANUEL

DECEMBER 22

OPENING PRAYER

O gracious Light,
pure brightness of the everliving Father in heaven,
O Jesus Christ, holy and blessed!
Now as we come to the setting of the sun,
and our eyes behold the vesper light,
we sing your praises, O God: Father, Son, and Holy Spirit.
You are worthy at all times to be praised by happy voices,
O Son of God, O Giver of life,
and to be glorified through all the worlds.

READINGS

Therefore the Lord himself will give you a sign. Look, the
young woman is with child and shall bear a son, and shall name
him Immanuel.

Isaiah 7:14

For the Lord is our judge, the Lord is our ruler,
the Lord is our king; he will save us.

Isaiah 33:22

41

Now the birth of Jesus the Messiah took place in this way. When his mother Mary had been engaged to Joseph, but before they lived together, she was found to be with child from the Holy Spirit. Her husband Joseph, being a righteous man and unwilling to expose her to public disgrace, planned to dismiss her quietly. But just when he had resolved to do this, an angel of the Lord appeared to him in a dream and said,

. . . "Joseph, son of David, do not be afraid to take Mary as your wife, for the child conceived in her is from the Holy Spirit. She will bear a son, and you are to name him Jesus, for he will save his people from their sins." All this took place to fulfil what had been spoken by the Lord through the prophet:

"Look, the virgin shall conceive and bear a son,
and they shall name him Emmanuel,"
which means, "God is with us."

Matthew 1:20-24

There is one lawgiver and judge who is able to save and to destroy.

James 4:12

THE SONG OF MARY

Antiphon: O Emmanuel, our King and Lawgiver, the Expected of the nations and the Savior of them all, O come and save us, O Lord our God.

My heart is overflowing with praise of my Lord,
my soul is full of joy in God my Savior.
For he has deigned to notice me, his humble servant and, after
this, all the people who ever shall be will call me the
happiest of women!
The one who can do all things has done great things for me—
oh, holy is his Name!
Truly, his mercy rests on those who fear him in every
generation.
He has shown the strength of his arm,
he has swept away the high and mighty.

He has set kings down from their thrones and lifted up the
humble.
He has satisfied the hungry with good things
and sent the rich away with empty hands.
Yes, he has helped Israel, his child:
he has remembered the mercy that he promised to our forefathers,
to Abraham and his sons for evermore!
Glory to the Father, and to the Son, and to the Holy Spirit:
as it was in the beginning, is now, and will be forever. Amen.

Antiphon: O Emmanuel, our King and Lawgiver, the Expected
of the nations and the Savior of them all, O come and save us,
O Lord our God.

THE LORD'S PRAYER

Our Father in heaven,
hallowed be your Name,
your kingdom come,
your will be done,
on earth as in heaven.
Give us today our daily bread.
Forgive us our sins
as we forgive those who sin against us.
Save us from the time of trial
and deliver us from evil.
For the kingdom, the power, and the glory are yours,
now and for ever. Amen.

MEDITATION

When we pray, O come, O come Emmanuel, we are asking that
God will indeed come to us in human flesh, that Christ's incarnation will be made real for us. This is a petition of hope and for
deliverance. It is a prayer that, had God not made the first move
toward us, we would not be able to utter. God does not remain
distant from us, but actually enters into our joys and sufferings.

In the words of a popular Christmas carol, ". . . And he feeleth for our sadness, And he shareth in our gladness. . . ."[1]

It is not unrealistic for us to ask where is God that there are poor and homeless, abused children, and babies born addicted to alcohol and other drugs. Too often we forget that God is poor and homeless, cowering with the child in the corner, or shaking in a newborn's crib. God's glory is seen in the helpless, the weak, the dying, the aged, the children, the brain-damaged—none are dispensable: each person is infinitely important to God. Each person is the one for whom Jesus was born and for whom Jesus died. Rather than ask why the innocent suffer or where God is when there is suffering, we need to ask ourselves how it is that we cause the innocent to suffer and what we can do to alleviate suffering. How much can we share of our own brokenness so that someone else can endure the otherwise unendurable? The way people know God is through us—we are here to make God's kingdom known to other people.

And it is only because Christ is Emmanuel—*God with us*—that Israel, and in fact all of us, are able to rejoice! It is when Christ comes as Emmanuel that the importance, vocation and dignity of every person will be restored.

O God with us,
   Emmanuel,
     whose law and life and rule are love;
You are, in fact, our only hope.
   Greed and injustice
     in the justice of the nations
discover us deep into poverty,
     starvation, corruption and war.
And into our homes sneak silent abuse
   and assault,
     incest and injury—
   a polite and private life of poverty,
     starvation, corruption and war.
Make no mistake—we
   don't know the slightest
   what we're asking you: to be saved

will be a costly bargain—
and one we hadn't fully reasoned on or planned.
Nevertheless,
   you are our only hope,
      O God with us,
Emmanuel.

CLOSING PRAYER

Eternal Father, you gave to your incarnate Son the holy name of Jesus to be the sign of our salvation: Plant in every heart, we pray, the love of him who is the Savior of the world, our Lord Jesus Christ; who lives and reigns with you and the Holy Spirit, one God, in glory everlasting. Amen.[2]

O   Vir-gin of vir   gins, * tell

us   how   shall   this be? For nei - ther be - fore

you was a - ny like   you   nor   shall

there   be   af - ter.   Daugh - ters of   Je - ru -

sa - lem,   why do   you mar - vel at   me? The

rit.

thing   which you   be - hold   is a   di - vine

mys - te - ry.

O VIRGIN

DECEMBER 23

OPENING PRAYER

O gracious Light,
pure brightness of the everliving Father in heaven,
O Jesus Christ, holy and blessed!
Now as we come to the setting of the sun,
and our eyes behold the vesper light,
we sing your praises, O God: Father, Son, and Holy Spirit.
You are worthy at all times to be praised by happy voices,
O Son of God, O Giver of life,
and to be glorified through all the worlds.

READINGS

The angel said to her, "Do not be afraid, Mary, for you have
found favor with God. And now, you will conceive in your
womb and bear a son, and you will name him Jesus. He will
be great and will be called Son of the Most High, and the Lord
God will give to him the throne of his ancestor David. He will
reign over the house of Jacob forever, and of his kingdom there
will be no end." Mary said to the angel, "How can this be, since
I am a virgin?" The angel said to her, "The Holy Spirit will come
upon you, and the power of the Most High will overshadow

you; therefore the child to be born will be holy; he will be called Son of God.''

When Elizabeth heard Mary's greeting, the child leaped in her womb. And Elizabeth was filled with the Holy Spirit and exclaimed with a loud cry, ''Blessed are you among women, and blessed is the fruit of your womb.''

Luke 1:41-42

And Mary said, ''My soul magnifies the Lord, and my spirit rejoices in God my Savior, for he has looked with favor on the lowliness of his servant. Surely, from now on all generations will call me blessed; for the Mighty One has done great things for me, and holy is his name. His mercy is for those who fear him from generation to generation.

Luke 1:46-50

THE SONG OF MARY

Antiphon: O Virgin of virgins, tell us how shall this be? For neither before you was any like you nor shall there be after. Daughters of Jerusalem, why do you marvel at me? The thing which you behold is a divine mystery.

My heart praises the Lord;
  my soul is glad because of God my Savior,
  for he has remembered me, his lowly servant!
From now on all people will call me happy,
  because of the great things the Mighty God has done for me.
His name is holy;
  from one generation to another
  he shows mercy to those who honor him.
He has stretched out his mighty arm
  and scattered the proud with all their plans.
He has brought down mighty kings from their thrones,
  and lifted up the lowly.
He has filled the hungry with good things,
  and the rich away with empty hands.

He has kept the promise he made to our ancestors,
and has come to the help of his servant Israel.
He has remembered to show mercy to Abraham
and all his descendants forever!
Glory to the Father, and to the Son, and to the Holy Spirit:
as it was in the beginning, is now, and will be forever. Amen.

Antiphon: O Virgin of virgins, tell us how shall this be? For neither before you was any like you nor shall there be after. Daughters of Jerusalem, why do you marvel at me? The thing which you behold is a divine mystery.

THE LORD'S PRAYER

Our Father in heaven,
hallowed be your Name,
your kingdom come,
your will be done,
on earth as in heaven.
Give us today our daily bread.
Forgive us our sins
as we forgive those who sin against us.
Save us from the time of trial
and deliver us from evil.
For the kingdom, the power, and the glory are yours,
now and for ever. Amen.

MEDITATION

Although this antiphon, unlike the others, is not addressed to Christ, it is nevertheless an attempt on our part to know and understand that which we worship. It is as though we are asking for a sharing into Mary's human insight and intuition in order to help us understand. But when all is said and done, God's incarnation must remain for us a mystery beyond human comprehension. We can imagine such love, but only imagine, for the depth and breadth of God's love for us is immeasurable— inestimable— by any standards that we have.

Perhaps, by drawing close to Mary, the God-bearer—*Theotokos* in Greek: she who gave birth to God—we will understand. But no, even then our "knowing" and "understanding" will always remain and require a leap of faith. God with us remains a divine mystery!

No wonder
  you might wonder, Mary—
It's an unheard of thing,
  an event beyond wondering,
    beyond imagining.
You're too young,
  too immature,
    unknown,
      too much a child.
It's never happened,
  can't happen,
    can't be—
      we don't understand it.
We don't apprehend,
  comprehend,
    or even want to think about it.
Oh, my sisters,
  why do you wonder?
  why do you marvel?
I'm not the wonder—
  I'm not the marvel—
I'm Mary, only me.
  The wonder, the marvel
    is God,
      God's gift,
        a mystery!

CLOSING PRAYER

O God, who wonderfully created, and yet more wonderfully restored, the dignity of human nature: Grant that we may share the divine life of him who humbled himself to share our humanity, your Son Jesus Christ; who lives and reigns with you, in the unity of the Holy Spirit, one God, for ever and ever. Amen.[1]

NOTES

1. *The Book of Common Prayer* (New York: The Church Hymnal Corporation, 1977) 395.
The Opening Prayer *(Phos hilaron)* and The Lord's Prayer for each day are from "Daily Evening Prayer: Rite II," *The Book of Common Prayer,* 118 and 121.
All Scripture quotations are from *The New Revised Standard Version.*

Introduction

1. *The Hymnal 1940* (New York: The Church Pension Fund, 1940). Used by permission.

December 16

Text for The Song of Mary *(Magnificat)* is from *The Book of Common Prayer,* 119.
1. Edward N. West, *The Far-Spent Night: Meditations on the Coming of Christ* (Greenwich, CT: The Seabury Press, 1960) 68.
2. *The Book of Common Prayer,* 231.

December 17

Text for The Song of Mary *(Magnificat)* is from the *Holy Bible, New International Version.* (International Bible Society, 1984) Used by permission of Zondervan Bible Publishers.
1. Diogenes Allen, *Three Outsiders* (Cambridge, MA: Cowley Publications, 1983) 13–14.
2. *The Book of Common Prayer,* 236.

December 18

Text of The Song of Mary *(Magnificat)* is from *The Bible, New Revised Standard Version* (Grand Rapids, MI: Zondervan Publishing House, 1993).
1. Charles deFoucauld, *Silent Pilgrimage To God,* trans. Jeremy Moiser (Maryknoll, NY: Orbis Books, 1974) 42.
2. *The Book of Common Prayer,* 230–231.

December 19

Text of The Song of Mary *(Magnificat)* is from *The Living Bible* (Wheaton, IL: Tyndale House Publishers, 1986).

1. Richard Atherton, *Summons To Serve* (London: Geoffrey Chapman, 1977) 3.

2. "O Come, O Come Emmanuel," trans. by T. A. Lacey. David Willcocks and John Rutter, eds., *100 Carols for Choirs* (Oxford: Oxford University Press, 1989) 230.

3. *The Book of Common Prayer*, 216.

December 20

Text for The Song of Mary *(Magnificat)* is from *The Jerusalem Bible* (Garden City, NY: Doubleday and Company, Inc., 1968).

1. West, *The Far-Spent Night*, 109–110.

2. "A Patre Unigenitus," trans. by Sr. Elise, CHS, 1995. Used by permission.

3. *The Book of Common Prayer*, 213.

December 21

Text for The Song of Mary *(Magnificat)* is from *The New English Bible* (Oxford: Oxford University Press, 1961).

1. Edward N. West, unpublished.

2. *The Book of Common Prayer*, 235.

December 22

Text for The Song of Mary *(Magnificat)* is from *The New Testament in Modern English*, trans. by J. B. Phillips (New York: The Macmillan Company, 1960).

1. C. F. Alexander, "Once in royal David's city." Willcocks and Rutter, eds., *100 Carols for Choirs*, 260.

2. *The Book of Common Prayer*, 213.

December 23

Text for The Song of Mary *(Magnificat)* is from *Good News Bible* (New York: American Bible Society, 1976).

1. *The Book of Common Prayer*, 252.

REFERENCES

Allen, Diogenes. *Three Outsiders.* Cambridge, MA: Cowley Publications, 1983.

Atherton, Richard. *Summons To Serve.* London: Geoffrey Chapman, 1987.

Breviarium ad Usum Sarum. London: Cambridge University Press, 1882.

The Bible, King James Version. New York, NY: Simon and Schuster, 1936.

The Book of Common Prayer. New York: Church Hymnal Corporation, 1977.

deFoucauld, Charles. *Silent Pilgrimage to God.* Trans. Jeremy Moiser. Maryknoll, NY: Orbis Books, 1974.

Good News Bible. New York: American Bible Society, 1976.

Guthrie, D., J. A. Motyer, A. M. Stibbs and D. J. Wiseman. eds. *The Eerdmans Bible Commentary.* Grand Rapids, MI: Wm. B. Eerdmans Publishing Co., 1970.

Heschel, Abraham J. *The Insecurity of Freedom: Essays on Human Existence.* New York: Farrar, Straus and Giroux, 1966.

Holy Bible, New International Version. Grand Rapids, MI: Zondervan Bible Publishers, 1984.

Holy Bible, New Revised Standard Version. Grand Rapids, MI: Zondervan Bible Publishers, 1993.

The Hours of Prayer. London: A. R. Mowbray and Company, 1961.

The Hymnal 1940. New York: The Church Pension Fund, 1940.

The Jerusalem Bible. Garden City, NY: Doubleday and Company, Inc., 1968.

The Living Bible. Wheaton, IL: Tyndale House Publishers, 1986.

Phillips, J. B., trans. *The New Testament in Modern English.* New York, NY: The Macmillan Company, 1960.

West, Edward N. *The Far-Spent Night: Meditations on the Coming of Christ.* Greenwich, CT: Seabury Press, 1960.

Willcocks, David, and John Rutter, eds. *100 Carols for Choirs.* Oxford: Oxford University Press, 1989.